Rewoven in the Dew

Rewoven in the Dew

Poems by

Elizabeth O'Rourke

Cover design by Shay Culligan
Cover image by Evie S. on Unsplash
Author photo by Cristina Lozito

ISBN: 979-8-90146-911-8
Library of Congress Control Number: 2026939125

Kelsay Books
502 South 1040 East, A-119
American Fork, Utah 84003
Kelsaybooks.com

for Seamus:
my favorite classmate

& for Mum:
to this day still mothering

My heart

keeps like tomatoes into September
like ticks with their heads burrowed in.

Contents

What Happens Inside

The snow was supposed to start
weeks ago.
Haven't you wanted to wake up
when the air is spacious
and the trains stay off the tracks?

There's a tune we'll hum then,
a wine we'll drink
and wide candles in glass
we'll light again.

I can stay inside for days
no shoes but slippers—both of us: all books and lips.

Honey

for Lori & Ruth

It sounds like a sister when they say it:
Honey, you brought the good blue cheese. Or
Hey hey don't forget your charger, hun, goodnight.
No one is chiding; this is not *toots,* not *ma'am,* not our reclaimed
bitch.
It has the sound of slipping into a stilled tub, the open-mouthed
vowels of wonder
of undulate
of sauvignon
of aria.
So when it's *Oh honey, I'll drive you there on the twenty fourth* or
Here's your coffee; careful, hun, it's hot or
Oh, I know. I know. Honey, I do,
It is protection running down the sides
covering the flanks, the hips—
all of us now sweet
shining.

Remembering Raftery

An Irish poet (1779–1835), author
of the poem "Cill Aodáin"

The last light in the upstairs bedroom was the best thing,
& the first few nights we slept readily
with the dog's head resting in the soft dip
between hip & rib.
We did things we never had:
counted five hoots lined up at the window at 3 in the morning,
gave each other long quiet kisses on the hill in the backyard.
I liked to watch the steam lift from my tea mug while the last of
    the night
combed the dark out of her hair.

There, we were an abundance:
of arms pushing paint rollers & hard bristled brushes,
of knees on tiles.
Hope draped us in deep-hued vestments.
After working we broke the bread & baked the pasta,
poured out in verbs our plans, dimensions & blueprints.

The house, we called Cill Aodáin, and it was true—
everything grew there.
I will look again every summer for the cornstalks,
for the mint underfoot.
There is patience in the seasons & a calm in the wait.

Complete the Living

This is what you have on your table:
a board with three slices of green apple,
a small piece of brie that has melted,
perhaps a damp ring where you continue
to place your glass down.

You have been walking all day with the dog—
his two steps to your one break of the leaf,
had wanted to come upon a gated stable of mares
shaking their manes and
clomping their beautiful nailed shoes.
Was that a circle of ferns you passed
while you looked up for the nesting owls?

It becomes difficult to notice everything;
now don't you find, it's all you can do while
having your dinner alone?
You must have understood
that you'd be asked to complete the living
on your own someday.

Custard

Nevermind, I said, the third time my husband said *what* from the living room after I called for help pulling the trashcan over to me.

Do I want him to nevermind—truly? So I can stand here separating eggs, broken yolky hands with the trashcan still in the corner?

No what, he says, *I just can't hear you.* No shit, I think and wonder how he and I do this only two rooms away.

Six weeks after we met, he moved to Ireland for five months—I remember because I have all the letters. None of them say *help me* or *nevermind.*

None of them swear under their papery breaths, and none of them are unable to hear me, even from that far away.

Before Children

I.

We have forgotten the days are divided.
We sit at night and eat our supper in low light,
following the sounds of forks to find each other's mouths.

Padding around on hardwood floors, opening and closing closet doors,
we're surprised to find our own coats are behind them—
that we're allowed to live here.

It's easy to repair something at a time like this:
to hear an E string is sharp,
its tiny fist lilting into the air,
to pull a fiddle string until it sounds clean.

This is the youngest we will ever be, here.
But we don't live alone;
our hawk's in the tree out back again.

II.

The trees out back have so many hands against the sky.
Out there with a Sunday pint
listing
hammock, tomatoes, bird feeder, sundial, rosemary, clothesline
for when the leaves come back.

That's enough for now.

XIII

for Seamus

There wasn't one thing that sold us on the house back then.
There was the spit of a yard, the reddish deck like a treehouse,
the promise of city friends sleeping over & breakfasts.
We set the table for two & cleared the yard for a garden.
We weren't nearly there yet: calculating the unexpected wait or
  due dates.
The foxlike dog joined us soon enough and
the chives became perennial: thirteen springs of their onion scent;
  their purple plumes
of garlicky flower sprinkled on supper; thirteen thrills of each
  inaugural falling snow;
the solstice sunset on the west facing patio.

Next spring when we walk by,
with others inside, we can say,
I loved (you in) that house.

Infertility

The house kept all our secrets the first winter:
folded them into dishtowels set softly in drawers,
made leafy nests for them in the backyard trails,
muffled their little sobs with smoothly drifting snowfalls.
A person had to hold my gaze during a greeting to suspect a
    problem because
I had learned & mastered the wide-eyed holiday hello, dissolving
    instantly into embraces.

I sometimes looked at my life spilling out of the bottom of a wet
    paper cup:
indistinguishable, falling drops pouring together
finding, always, the spaces between my bowled fingers and I
    carried on like this.

Working Against

There are things my mother loves:
in particular, a cocktail I make for her called *Juice of a Few Flowers*
and looking for work suits the rainy day after Labor Day, consigning in Harwich.
The phone has been cold between us because another thing she loves is
grandchildren and one thing I know she'll hate is a thin and frightened daughter
with a thinner and inhospitable uterine lining.

There are viscous and slick items to fight this:
castor oil applied to the abdomen, soaking of the feet nightly, needles in the webbing of the fingers,
blueberries in yogurt, cinnamon, walnuts with avocado, gelato, muddy herbs steeped in boiling water,
meditation or a concentration on breathing,
breathing,
less lengthy running routes, folic acid in tea because otherwise the sicky sweetness causes nausea:

the beginning of trying forever to make more & more of myself.

Infertility II

I drive alone thirty minutes to the train station for our rainy
reunion,
stopping along the way, early, to have a pint of beer & each
swallow is the mellow, slowly crawling feeling of another
weekend together: just us.
Looking up from my glass, my coaster—three more minutes until
I'm late to greet him on the platform:
one for the Christmas party we evaded since everyone is
expecting;
two for Mum who phones most days to test the waters;
three for the baby and her initial, busy, cellular burrowing;
for her choosing me,
& for my unknowing.

Diadhánach

Translation of the word diadhánach is credited to Manchán Magan (1970–2025) during his interview in the short film "The Search for John James Burns."

The nurse took you for cleaning and measuring while I called,
"May I have her back now?" again, then again, because
at once the waters we had lived in were gone; now lands and
hands between us,
and I wanted everything touching.

There were twelve hours of the scythe to your path and the teary
crippling.
I could not listen to songs with words.
My legs were shifted by others.
I forgot names of things—a blanket, cup, or screen.
I opened every rib to find a breath.

The morning pushed back the sheets and peeked through the
window corners.
It was the day you were born—alive and crying.

Diadhánach (Irish): the lonesomeness of the cow bereft of her
calf.
My longing for you, Hope, now yours.

We are stone-written: the way the rain always stops,
the way the beach becomes wide again,
the webs, rewoven in the dew.

afterbirth

if you get chased, he likes you. use your fingernail to imbed an x on the top of the mosquito bite so it doesn't itch any more. don't push the Ouija board let it do its work. if the dandelion rubs yellow into your palm the plague will get you. turn the lights out and stare hard into the mirror. Bloody Mary'll come it's terrifying. blast yourself with cold water at the end of your shower for shiny hair. the sharks can smell your blood so don't swim deep on your period. lift your shoulders and tilt them forward that's how you can see the bones for a picture. turn a little sideways too.

try to pee every time after sex. you can sate your hunger for an hour with lifesavers or certs. liquor before beer in the clear. don't give the milk away for free; make him want the cow. count fourteen days after you start bleeding. don't do it then. eventually, do it then. don't take the sliced meat at the risk of listeria. stay quiet for sixty seconds a day and count the movements. stay quiet. start stool softener a few weeks before you're due. you should still be having sex. and still peeing afterwards. come in when the contractions are two minutes apart. lie there.

nothing about the third stage of labor, though, the surprise second delivery. the way the contractions continue afterwards: aftershock of shudders. in your premature triumph the doctor still seated by your raised feet. the placenta and its bloodied weight detaching itself from inside you with a tissue tear. the pushing still ahead when you were counting so heavily on having already reached the end. the entire grown organ a necessary but unexpected loss. the soft plop of it. the twisted branch where it rooted. the final emptying that came with no warning.

The Second Fall

Late morning, we rock in her small blue room with our bellies
  pressed together.
She slows her head nodding, stops
pointing at the window when the trains rumble through.
I cup her diapered bottom with both my hands
(my mother must have done this),
trace her elbow crease, her wrist.

Her body is soft and quiet now; her marvelous
organs busily expanding, purifying
automatically. I drop my face nearer to her mouth to smell the air
  she pushes out
(my mother must have done this).

I, who consider murmurations majesty;
I, who can dissolve in the Eucharistic Prayer: that terror, that trust;
I, who am broken open each day at eleven thirty naptime;
(&, my mother must have done *this*)
wait a moment on the other side of my daughter's closed door
  facing it.

How I Learned

There were things that went well.
There was the simple, sweet act on the certain night that was the perfect marriage of matter.
There was the correct, hospitable temperature and the hopeful resting afterwards.
There was the decided-upon day to tell, the expected elation and prenatals nightly.
Again, the hopeful resting.
There were the quiet murmurs and whirs of the ultrasound machine and the tiny spinning spinning spinning in the heart space.
There was so much limeade and the thin pizza with ricotta and olives.
There were the vials of deep maroon blood that came back from a lab heralding the other things that were going well:
our Rh factors were compatible, my hCG levels doubled appropriately, I didn't appear anemic.
There was a lavender lotion Seamus rubbed into the soles of my feet each evening
and the muted thuds of the child's knees against my abdomen after mint ice cream in a mug.
There was an undeniable love for the strangeness and familiarity of the child.
There were the ten or so minutes at the end of my yoga class when I could lie flat and put my hands on the child,
tap tapping gently on what I assumed was the bottom or lower back.
There were rosemary crackers and trips out for more limeade.

There was a calm when I called my mother from my parking spot
after the doctor explained about the mass in the child's lung.
There was the way I got to the station for Seamus.
There were still things inside the child that were going well.
The heart continued its spinning even as it was pushed out of
place.
The trachea remained unpinched and available for intubation.
The other lung grew on and on.
A straightforward amniocentesis showed the abnormal growth as
an isolated phenomenon.
We considered this a bright spot.
There was the way Estanya, my favorite ultrasound technician,
some weeks smiled tenderly and told me the mass wasn't
measuring any larger.
There was the way it rained almost every Friday that summer, so
after we arrived home from the hospital I could sleep well for
an hour or two,
with a pillow between my knees and the window by our
headboard open.
There was the morning my older daughter, almost three and eating
oatmeal said,
"I miss the baby, Mum," and that went well because I knew
exactly what she intended
and I felt ready, too.

The Places Walkable from Morgan Stanley Children's Hospital

The lobby café sells tea, and if you like Earl Grey in the afternoon it's available. Across Broadway is the Au Bon Pain, quite new, so it's not a shock to go from the sterility of the PICU to the shining tiles and eager newly-hired, wiping everything. Carrot Top Bakery means just the one crosswalk commute and is open early on Mother's Day if you want a breakfast sandwich with sausage after the hospital's mass in the non-denominational chapel. You can get cupcakes for the mothers who are nurses and working. Further away, walking the winding sidewalk through neighborhoods filled with folks without visitor passes is the restaurant with its uneven flooring and local art blaring on the walls. You can say you're out for coffee and also get a red wine in a glass water cup if it seems you might not be able to go home again that day. You can make it one and a half city blocks to Crazy Annie's for takeout in a rainstorm in three minutes if the lights are in your favor, and that will feel like a victory.

At Home with It

For a few weeks Sinéad was home
with a three-inch long, portable chest tube in her left flank,
benignly referred to by her doctors as her *valve.*

Twice daily on her changing table, I'd twist a syringe
onto the base of it
and pull back
collecting the thick yellow liquid
that had leaked from her pleural space.

It looked so close
to colostrum: that golden liquid newborns extract
the first few nursing days.
I was conflicted pouring it down the sink.

Fifteen days she and I did this.
Morning: twist, pull, kiss, pour out, zip up her sleeper.
Evening: twist, pull, kiss, pour out, zip up her sleeper.
We were at home with it.

The Season

The reason you got so angry is because you didn't want to read
the book,
& I wanted to because, the day after Halloween,
I had brought all the Thanksgiving books to replace the spooky
ones.

I took them from the carefully, seasonally arranged shelf,
brought them from the playroom to the living room by the big
reading chair,
and that had made me feel accomplished.

When you rebuked again, I slapped a book on my lap.
That was not instructive nor was
introducing you to the word *ungrateful.* I'm sorry

a dozen times a day, at least,
while you're being five and pressing the places on me
that will chatter my jaw or cause me to put my forehead

against the back of my bedroom door while you wait on the other
side.
Sometimes, you grit your teeth and hiss, "stop crying" at your
toddler sister and now,
thirteen times today I am sorry. Let me approach the median.

I can remember to French braid your hair at the sink in the
    morning
with deft gentleness, pulling your swivel chair onto the bathroom
    tile,
affecting the accent that makes you hard-smile,

pretending to be your ridiculous hairstylist who remembers all
    your cousins' names.
I can walk down our narrow stairwell and stop,
wait patiently at the side when, again,
you ask to be the leader today.

I can cut your lunch into small diagonals, like sails, *like Nana
    does, Mama.*
I can wield the dull knife with patience.

Revisitation

They come through you; but not from you.
And though they are with you, yet they belong not to you.
—Kahlil Gibran

On Tuesday of the second week in November, mine stopped
nursing, and asked only twice,
sweetly, tugging at the top of my nightgown and saying softly,
"mum mum."
It's a breakaway: the ceasing; the body back to yourself;
exhaustion ticked down an ounce;
button-down sweaters, shirts with slits at the sides
to the back of the closet.

Thanksgiving brought my sister-in-law and her three-week-old:
taking their breaks every other hour & nestled into one another
with Grace gulping.
I know how Meghan takes her tea so I was close by a fair bit.

It took those two days only, my occasional holding & intermittent
rocking of Grace,
for my milk to come back in,
leading me to the bath, pressing from the top down,
releasing plumes in the tub.
Not mine. Through me, but not mine.

Office Hours

The drafting table in the sunny back basement,
installed for writing during naptime, library lectures,
and quiet date-at-home pints & the crossword,
is barely two and a half feet high: just right
for her toddler nose to rest on, rising and shifting gently
as she chews raisin after raisin and tells me
she loves them.
It's her second tiny red box of the day, but it's Friday
and it makes her happy. God knows
it's anything for her
spitty grin, her fingernail triumphantly dislodging
the wetted skin of the once-grape from a molar,
the perfection of her tiny parts in harmony
doing work.

I'm holding the tooth

where she held it to tug it out and I'm tracing the light ridge of her
plaque:
five of her very own birthday cakes, melting berry popsicles and
drips down her knuckles,
Halloween Reese's, Christmas candy canes, snow day hot cocoas.

This bit of bone tucked below her gums while she bleated,
rooted blindly when I longed so much to sleep, to drink
quiet tea, to choose thoughtfully a brie in the cheese aisle.

This miniature mighty calcium deposit back then breaking
her gums, pinking her cheeks, even fevering her,
later allowing: soft eggs; roasted, cooled, & quartered sweet
potatoes;
bits of ripe nectarine devoid of their skins; sometimes orange
sherbet.

She has grown it & used it & shed it.
In my hand, the piece of her we made: too small now for her
lengthening jaw,
for the way her mouth moves pronouncing digraphs, articulating
consonants,
the kisses she will give us with some bits missing.

Rye YMCA

The senior aquatics class lets out Mondays about eleven in the
morning,
so most of the ladies are naked or towel clad in the locker room by
half past,
maneuvering around one another carefully,
dripping a bit on each other's shoulders and tugging at lockers.
The oils for feet! The plastic Ziplocs for every possible potion!

I love to watch them, I have to—
their soft folds, the pillowy parts that lead to knees, to unexpected
pink toenails,
a rogue soap sud on the back of an arm, which takes a particular
effort not to brush away.
So warm in that room, such surrounding comfort.
I can open my pores in the heat, absorb the motherly molecules
and take them for the week.

Body. Woman.

Pushed into and pushed
against. It is sexy when
pressed; sexier when slender;
best, actually, when
impossibly small.

Passed over and handed
down. It is lesser after being
spent in. Tally how many
went in. Bagged. Tagged.
Ride. Tried.

Pushed out of and pressed
against. It is best when
growing (someone), with
milk flowing, when glowing
and holding. Beautiful when
broken down like that.

Grazed against and waist-
held. Large hands on the
small of the back, small talk
largely close to the face.
Pretty little bits: necklace
links and ringlets to be
fingered.

Crouched over and hurried along. Nuisances in parking lots. Slack skin, unwanted parts, awake at night from running hot. Experts on the expiration.

Lockdown Practice

for Hope in 2019

"Inside our cubbies," she tells me in a whisper when we discuss
the drill Mrs. Blaney's kindergarten class did on Tuesday.

Lights flicked off and door latched, all twenty-one sealed their lips
and filed quietly across the alphabet rug to the back wall:

tiny Mary Janes tiptoeing on A, apple, double knotted gym day
sneakers scurrying over B, boat.

They become silent versions of their small selves, reverent in the
unaccustomed midday dimness and

intent on the title: Most Quiet Classroom.

They do this, she says, so no danger in the hallway knows they're
in there.

Danger, simply, like that: inanimate, without eyes, shoulders,
beating heart, rifle.

"And Mum, in the cubbies," she revisits, "you cannot say one
single word, even if you are next to your very best friend,

even if you really want to."

The Game After Dinner

The noise is coming from my father,
who has been out back with the leaf blower,
leaf blowing bits of mulch or rogue twigs
off his neat stone patio.
Now he has brought it inside.
It's cordless. It's running on a battery or oil & gas or
whatever he loads it with, ticking through his to-do list
in the cool & quiet garage.
So he has it by the door to the basement & blows it
in short then long Morse-like bursts
onto the pajamaed bodies of my daughter & nephew.
They grab & laugh at one another, overcome by the safe
intensity of the squalls.

The noise is also coming from them, shrieking & gulping
through thick bouts of deep laughter,
losing their breath a moment when my father
aims, briefly, at their faces.
My nephew doubles over, recovering.
My daughter turns, letting the air blasts lift
the curls off the back of her neck
when she needs a break.
She is a spinning flash of flannel with her eyes closed.
She is the pinwheel my father can set dancing with a breeze.

Summer of

always something:
Sinéad's surgery at seven months old;
the summer my cousin in his tragedy could not listen to the rest of us;
the summer my mother, with a long exasperated and lengthy sigh
at last, let me shave my legs after the boys in camp for weeks
refused to be in a boat with me.

This summer my oldest, with trepidation
lifts beetles out of the pool, inspecting their wings for damage
their tiny sticky legs for any small movement.

She mourns the still, breathily rejoices in the still-moving,
goes in each time, hand open
cupping both water and creature.

I have done small things

today: have threaded the needle's eye with the current favorite
seafoam spool, have closed up
the tear where the down spilled out of my daughter's winter coat,
have dragged
the heavy bags back to the feeders lofting them on my shoulder
and waited
for the pouring sound to climb its rasping octave and the seed to
reach the brim, have taken
a moment midday to remind myself of my mother's legs pedaling
her bike to the post office on the backroads, have poured
water on the roots of the olive tree and the Meyer lemon tree who
can't articulate their needs, have whispered
beautiful boy to my old and sleeping dog, his damp nose in a slice
of sunlight, have swept
sweaty curls off temples no bigger than a rose petal with a
particular kindness, have watched
the designated ant bring the body of the dead in its arms all the
way along the baseboard, have given
the onions their time to weep in the butter the rice its space to
toast, have folded
the last of the day into neat and quiet piles of dishtowels, of
matched and nestled socks.

Elegy for Kristelle

1980–2025

i

Dearly beloved, to whom it may concern,
we are gathered here today.
In peace, let us take our sister
to her place of rest.

ii

Dear, loved sister,
gather peace, take rest.
In our concern we . . .
To whom are . . .?

iii

Take her peace to us
who gather here, dear place.
Rest our concern today.
May it be love we let in.

iv

Red rest in place of our dear sister—
Today we, in concern, gather.
Let it take us.

v

Let us love our sister,
once here,
in her place of rest today.

vi

We gather in peace
to place our sister to rest
who once let us be hers.

Checkup

The dentist has his fingers
    by my mouth now
        pushing around methodically.
Whereas ten minutes ago
    he'd used them to wrap mine in the waiting room
        and then hold them like that.
He's new at the practice
    so greeted me with a surge of smile,
        of hyperfocus and introductions.
I've been with two men, ever
    and am in the sixteenth year
        of my marriage to the second.
In my recline here
    there is no place to look
        but to his eyes above his mask.
This is a loophole
    which is to say a small opening
        to allow observation, light, air.

Breakaway

A sonnet for Leo

When it was time the vet and her tech were
the lifesavers: tissues and whispered words
gentle explanations about the way
each particular injection would work.
(Sedation comes first and then the vial
inducing anesthetic overdose.)
They set up the oversized bed right there
on the exam room floor where he waited.

What is the gentlest way to fall asleep?
Late afternoon beams through a high window?
The perfect curve of the linked vertebrae?
Imagine for him it was just like that.
His heartbeat and its predicted slowing:
the quiet part you sometimes hear mid-song.

The Wise Decision

1 Kings 3:16–28

S'il y en a pour un, il y en a pour deux.
—French proverb

My body betrayed me. It was the exhaustion—the
bones as stone, weary exhaustion—I had
pushed and torn and wailed and bled and his need
was immediate and relentless and trust me
I loved him—him with his forehead wisps and perfect
curved upper lip—him with his little hungry
squalls. I made his milk I gave him his milk daylong,
nightlong, daylong. My body betrayed me I
was too tired.

And in the part of the night only we knew, where
we met and rocked and I whispered to him that
he was all the sides of the World and the space
around it as well, in that part on that night it
was at once just me (again) so soon and when I say
my body betrayed me, it betrayed him (who
was me after all).

Pulled him gently out from under me already
knowing and swallowed swallowed my scream. I
gave him his final salty rinse and must have
put my feet on the clay and padded around—so
tired—so slowly—and it must have been when
I walked by the other room and heard that
mewling. Same wisps same heft.
Blessed changeling.

For as long as I remember everything is taken
from me (over and over) now I am empty again.
As I remember I didn't have a word in any of it. I am
so tired my body betrayed me. If there is
enough for one there is enough for two,
as is said.

The Synoptic Reason

After Mark 5: 24–34

The bleeding was relentless and went on so long:
dark heavy clots, bright red streams, around the clock flow,
through the burlap folded over onto itself
turning tepid bathwater an unsettling
pink, swirling tendriling streams of it when she ran
her fingers through the water in between her thighs.
Years, in fact, twelve of them always replenishing—
by way of rinsed carrot greens (anything leafy)
brown boiled lentils (sometimes, blessedly, in broth)
on a lucky day maybe a few ripe cherries
or a raspberry or two (carefully or else
that could mean more blood, except from her fingertips).
All of those men who saw her, looked and urgently
ungently prodded, each time taking a treasured
denarius, and then giving no pronouncement.
So on His pass through town and her path into the
sweating teeming crowd, a quick nimble grasp of His
dusty hem did it—the stoppage: like the dried leaves
of her thyme hanging upside down over the sill;
like the drops into the wooden bucket at last
quiet once the shaking thunder sounds far away;
like the street gutters dry and dusty enough for
the children to walk barefoot along; the woman
nearly sick to death from the leeching of herself.
It was the body failing and someone turning
toward it. First, though, that body reaching to receive.
When they say He came to her and she was fearful,
she was: for her life. And when they say she trembled
she did: from the final and exquisite relief.

Acknowledgments

I give special thanks to the following publications and readers there who chose to feature my poems before they became a part of this whole:

MER Literary: "I Have Done Small Things"

On Being: "Complete the Living," "Before Children"

The Westchester Review: "XIII," "How I Learned"

Writing Fire: An Anthology Celebrating the Power of Women's Words: "Diadhánach," "Remembering Raftery"

I sit with gratitude for writers and teachers who have walked alongside me in this beautiful practice—to poets who have passed & who continue to shape me as well as those in whose midst I've been lucky enough to grow: Victoria Redel, Marie Howe, Suzanne Gardinier, Pádraig Ó'Tuama, Kay Cosgrove, Sara Cappell Thomason, and Kevin Devaney, among many.

I am lucky to work with a group of formidable poets in The Poetry Craft Collective. Melissa, Anne, Ellen, Linda, Marjorie, Terrie, and Virginia: the Monday morning magic is fuel. The scaffolding we have built withstands all literary weather.

Libraries are necessary and safe spaces for all. I am honored to be the poetry teacher at mine: the Mamaroneck Public Library in New York. Thank you to the staff there, especially Trish and Amy, for allowing me the use of the community room and the garden for all those Friday afternoons with poets and patrons and for helping to get the word out. You. Are. Vital.

To fellow lovers of the work and word I get to call friends: Ruthie, Lori, Cristina, Pei-Ling & Aubrey who keep the candle lit. To Jacq who saw how the poet part of me was so much of my makeup. Thank you for reading with heart and tears.

My family has quietly and sometimes not so quietly celebrated alongside me as I do what I love, which for the last twelve years has been writing these poems. Mum and Dad, you have been constant, which is a gift. Bri, so much of how I see & mother is from traveling under your wing. Pat, I have needed your levity & breeze in many pockets of time while sorting through these experiences.

Before I tuck this in, to my daughters Hope and Sinéad: you made and continue to make my life like some sort of prize I did not know I was up for. I will never understand how I was picked for this stunning lifetime with you. Seamus, you are the reason why this book exists, the reason why my heart can feel such safe love, the reason why I want to record everything: so that there is confirmation of what is possible when folks love like this. I love you.

About the Author

Elizabeth O'Rourke's poetry is featured in Krista Tippett's "On Being" blog, *Mom Egg Review, Westchester Review,* and in the anthology *Writing Fire.* She studied at Boston College and received an MFA from Sarah Lawrence College. She is the poetry teacher at Mamaroneck Public Library and serves as the co-chair of the Village of Mamaroneck Arts Council.

Born outside of Boston to an Irish Catholic family, much of her writing focuses on the sacredness and mysticism of her daily encounters with the world and what it asks of her. Elizabeth reads and writes at home in Mamaroneck, NY and in Great Barrington, MA with her husband while caring for her young daughters Hope and Sinéad.

www.ingramcontent.com/pod-product-compliance
Lightning Source LLC
LaVergne TN
LVHW090537110826
845146LV00003B/1150
9798901469118